This book belongs to

●

If found, please contact

●

notes on mindful creative life

pause, breathe and grow

notes on mindful creative life

Radim Malinic

Brand Nu

First published in the United Kingdom
in 2020 by Brand Nu Limited,
www.brandnu.co.uk

**Pause, breathe and grow –
Notes on mindful creative life**
Copyright ©2020 Radim Malinic

1 2 3 4 5 6 7

Editor Emily Gosling

Meditation Content Contributor
Adiba Osmani

Visual Artist Tamas Arpadi

Creative direction and design
Radim Malinic

British Library Cataloguing-in-
Publication Data A catalogue record
for this book is available from
the British Library

ISBN 978-0-9935400-2-8 [Print]
ISBN 978-0-9935400-9-7 [Ebook]

Made in London, England

Printed by Park Communications
on FSC® certified paper. Park
works to the EMAS standard and its
Environmental Management System
is certified to ISO 14001.

This publication has been manufactured
using 100% offshore wind electricity
sourced from UK wind.

100% of the inks used are vegetable
oil based, 95% of press chemicals are
recycled for further use and, on average
99% of any waste associated with this
production will be recycled and the
remaining 1% used to generate energy.

This book is printed on Edixion
Offset paper made of material from
well-managed, FSC®-certified forests
and other controlled sources.

This is a certified climate neutral print
product for which carbon emissions
have been calculated and offset by
supporting recognised carbon offset
projects. The carbon offset projects
are audited and certified according
to international standards and
demonstrably reduce emissions.
The climate neutral label includes
a unique ID number specific to this
product which can be tracked at
www.climatepartner.com, giving
details of the carbon offsetting process
including information on the emissions
volume and the carbon offset project
being supported.

To find out more about this
publication or the author, visit
brandnu.co.uk
bookofideas.co.uk
pausebreathegrow.com

content

before you begin ...

Pause, Breathe and Grow was created to help its readers become more present, and in doing so, aid the flow of ideas and creativity. The prompts shared here are those which I've personally found helpful over the years, and I sincerely hope you enjoy your life and career more fully as you work through them.

The suggestions in this book are not intended as therapy for any health issues, mental or physical. If you are experiencing any such issues, or feel you might be, please seek professional medical advice. If you find any of the exercises here mentally or physically uncomfortable, please don't do them.

how to use this book

The pages of this book are designed to help you put each prompt into action, and encourage you to develop the suggestions into ongoing habits that you can easily track.

The prompt pages appear in chunks of seven, meaning that there's one prompt every day for a week. Each weekly section is then followed by a blank page for your summary notes and reflections as you look back over the past seven days. You'll find a total of sixteen sections spanning the book's three main chapters—titled Pause, Breathe and Grow—meaning there are enough prompts here to carry out a different one each day for sixteen weeks.

The pages are designed so that you can jot down the date you start each prompt. At the bottom of each page you'll find "habit tracker" dots (•) to tick off each time you manage to complete and then repeat each exercise, as well as a "mood tracker" for marking how you feel in general throughout each day. I'd suggest that you use an upwards arrow (✔) to denote a good mood, a dash for average (—) and a downwards arrow to indicate a low mood (✘). There's nothing to stop you from drawing any other signs, though (smiley or sad faces, for instance.)

Also at the bottom of each page is a section to note your sleep times, (☀ : ☾) meaning that as you work through the book you can track how much rest you're getting and how those habits change across the sixteen weeks. Finally, the bottom line encourages you to write down one thing you were grateful for each day.

What you put on the pages will vary with each prompt. Broadly speaking, the blank lines should be used to list how you're achieving or how you plan to achieve the directive—perhaps how easy or challenging you're finding it, how far you've felt it's been helpful and any other reflections or observations as you work your way through the book. These notes can be made both on the first day you start working on each prompt, and when you revisit them as and when they become relevant to your life and work further down the line.

introduction

Notes on mindful creative life is a collection of thought-provoking prompts that encourage you to unplug from the world for a moment. These suggestions gently steer you out of the fast lane, and help you take a detour from the endless highway we all too often find ourselves speeding down. Moving so fast tends to mean travelling on autopilot, and struggling to process the blur of thoughts and images that rapidly fade into the distance. This book helps you to slow down and make sense of that blur by sharpening how you see your working methods and career goals.

The exercises in this journal are drawn from the things that have helped me deal with the day-to-day pressures of running a creative business, as well as my experiences in tackling the ups and downs of life more generally. The most significant thing that's led me to living a happier and more creatively satisfying existence is learning to approach all aspects of my life mindfully. All the prompts in Pause, Breathe and Grow are based on the techniques that I've used in combination with one another, and which have led to a more present life.

We can all find a better balance between work, life and rest by focusing on the things we know are most important to us and yet we're aware we neglect. Many of us feel that we don't work enough, while also feeling we don't get a break or devote enough time to the people we love. I've run myself into the ground so many times in the past because I was lacking a clear sense of structure. It can be easy to feel we have to work all hours of the day. It's tempting to fight the fatigue and stress that arises from doing that with things that only make matters worse, like running on caffeine and sugar, losing sleep or pouring a couple more glasses of wine. Significant, long-term changes are just the sum of numerous small but powerful steps. Often we don't notice the incremental progress we're making until we see tangible effects. Building new, more mindful habits isn't always easy, but trust in yourself that you're improving—the results just might not be immediate.

While friends and family can offer an invaluable support network, the desire to truly change has to come from within us. Doing something differently can feel like an inconvenience, but just two minutes today, and the next day, and the ones after that make for a lifetime of positive change. Be kind to yourself—allow your mind the space it needs to enjoy the present moment, get perspective on the past and live a better future.

a mindful way of living

It goes without saying that modern life is filled with a staggering number of gadgets and tools that promise to save us time and make things generally easier. We have endless information at our fingertips, and digital diaries show us what each day looks like and notify us where we've got to be and when. Then there's the step counters; fridges that tell us when the milk's run out; invoicing software; sat navs; as well trackers for our sleep patterns and, somewhat ironically, our screen time.

These tools are a double-edged sword, though. However helpful they might seem, they let our brains slip into a sort of autopilot. Why bother to really pay attention when something else is doing most of the thinking? It's all too easy to find ourselves having arrived somewhere with absolutely no idea how we got there. Consider the mindful way as the paper map equivalent to a digital sat nav. It's up to you to define your destination and route, and mark off checkpoints along the way to make sure you're sticking to your path. With a paper map however, you consciously find the prompts and direction—an app isn't going to do it for you. In order to not get lost, you have to concentrate. You will know at each junction or bend in the road where you are at that precise moment, and if you meander from the route, you have to carefully find your way back.

A mindful approach means working to stay in each present moment; using all of our inbuilt senses to process exactly what's happening. It forces you to see the world anew, taking in everything it can possibly tell us. It puts aside first person narratives and invites an all-encompassing, more richly detailed perspective. By actively working to become more present, we engage our minds and discover more creative ways of navigating the world. In turn, our stress levels drop and our anxieties become more manageable. Creative block is less frequent and less terrifying. By helping us see the world more clearly, mindfulness aids the way we retain memories and shows us the little things that have helped us get where we are. Those insights help us sharpen our vision of the future—one we feel more positive about.

breathing exercise

Find a comfortable place to sit where you can be undisturbed for about ten minutes. Feel free to use a chair, sitting with both feet on the floor, or sit cross-legged on a bed or the floor if you prefer. Keep your back relaxed and supported.

Gently close your eyes, and start to take in all the sounds around you. The sounds will change, they'll come and go: just notice that they are there, and be content to keep them in the background. Then start to notice how you're breathing. Without changing your breathing in any way, cast your mental gaze on the breath. Notice how it feels as you breathe in, where the breath travels to, which parts of the body it moves, its rhythm, its pace and how it feels as it leaves the body. Settle into this gazing and maintain your relaxed, curious attention on your breathing for a couple of minutes.

Now slowly take a deep breath in, filling your lungs and the belly. Hold the breath for a second, then slowly exhale in three increments: exhale a little then pause, exhale a little more then pause again, and then finally exhale again, this time fully. Take a pause, allowing your breathing to resume its natural rhythm. Do this intentional incremental breathing a couple more times; breathing in slowly, fully, deeply, and exhaling in three increments, pausing between each. With each exhalation notice how your body also drops further into the seat—how your shoulders let go a little, and the muscles gradually surrender their tension.

Now resume following your body's normal breathing for a couple of minutes, resting with its familiarity and comfort. Slowly bring yourself back to the space you are in: start to notice the sounds around you, and gently open your eyes. How do you feel? A simple breathing exercise like this slows us right down, brings us into the present and helps ground our attention fully into this moment.

by **Adiba Osmani**

Download an audio version of this meditation - see page 192

pause

Just as a roaring fire starts with a miniscule spark, any change we want to make in life starts with a single second in which we purposely decide to take a new approach. In that moment, we actively move away from repeating the same mistakes.

This section shows you the way to work towards a more mindful way of life—pausing to stop doing and thinking for a moment, tuning in to your surroundings and slowing right down.

The following pages of prompts will encourage you to strip back the multiple thoughts that fight for attention and find clarity of mind in the here and now. Things will make a lot more sense when you take time to step off the merry-go-round of life for a moment and do something just for you. By allowing yourself to pause, you move towards an existence characterised by stability, and in which you're the one in full control of your thoughts and actions.

Work, play, rest

Look at how you balance your time between working, having fun (hobbies, family time, exercise, watching films and so on) and resting. It might be time to reevaluate where your hours go. An imperfect rule of thumb would be aiming to spend around a third of the time you have on each of these three things. Rest and downtime away from work are vital.

Write down your current split between work, rest and play
(eg. 50% work, 30% sleep, 20% play) and track how that averages out over a week

Habit tracker   •   •   •   •   •   •   •   •   •

Mood tracker   ☀   🌙   Sleep   ☀   :   🌙   :

Today, I am greatful for .....

Take the long route

One day each week, give yourself extra time to get to work and back and take a different, slower route. Give yourself enough spare minutes to make it feel as though you're simply out and about, instead of pushing for a personal commute speed record. This can put the rest of the day in a totally different light.

Plan your new route here

Habit tracker   •   •   •   •   •   •   •   •   •

Mood tracker   ☀   🌙   Sleep   ☀   :   🌙   :

Today, I am greatful for .....

Plant life

Studies have suggested that looking after a plant can help you live longer. The act of taking care of a plant brings about extra focus and meaning to our days. Even for those of us who've never been particularly green-fingered, it's worth buying a plant and seeing how the simple act of watering it and seeing it grow can make a real difference.

Research the plants that might fit into your life
and home and list them here

_____

_____

_____

_____

_____

_____

_____

_____

_____

_____

_____

_____

_____

_____

Habit tracker   •   •   •   •   •   •   •   •   •

Mood tracker   ☀   🌙   Sleep   ☀   :   🌙   :

Today, I am greatful for .....

Free time guilt

When we're obsessive about our craft, it's hard not to go in head first every day and try to squeeze in as many hours as possible. Having an hour or two off is no reason to give yourself grief. Make a small cognitive shift to let go of the guilt, and remember the importance of balancing work time and downtime.

`Make a note of how you spend your downtime`

Habit tracker   •   •   •   •   •   •   •   •   •

Mood tracker   ☀   ☾   Sleep   ☀   :   ☾   :

Today, I am greatful for .....

Listen, don't just hear

An anxiety to make sure that we're heard—to prove ourselves, even—can make us feel we need to hold a conversation, even to the point of trying to end someone else's sentences by haphazardly guessing at what they mean to say. That's not a true conversation, in that we're not actually listening, and it's highly unlikely we really understand what's being said to us. Listen, pause and think before you reply.

Note down how you make yourself listen before you speak

Habit tracker   •   •   •   •   •   •   •   •   •

Mood tracker   ☀   ☾   Sleep   ☀   :   ☾   :

Today, I am greatful for .....

The "impossible" day off

It might feel as though your entire business will collapse if you're not checking your emails ten times an hour. It won't: when you do take a break, everything really will be fine the following day and you'll feel all the better for having some time off. Be sure to build days off into your schedule, and enjoy them.

What will you do on your day off?

Make a list

Habit tracker   •   •   •   •   •   •   •   •   •

Mood tracker   ☀   🌙   Sleep   ☀   :   🌙   :

Today, I am greatful for .....

Reconnect the dots

Sometimes we need to remind ourselves how we got to where we are now. Our interests, inspirations and creative methods are changing all the time. Look back at your journey so far and reconnect the dots. Remind yourself how all of these various elements made you feel and helped drive you forward.

Write down hobbies, interests and creative methods you've previously enjoyed

---

Habit tracker   •   •   •   •   •   •   •   •   •

Mood tracker   ☀   🌙   Sleep   ☀   :   🌙   :

Today, I am greatful for .....

Notes and reflections

Sketch it out

You know the random doodles you find yourself absent-mindedly making when you're on the phone? Try making those same sort of sketches—ones that don't have to have a beginning or an end—but as a conscious exercise rather than an adjunct to a phone call. Set aside a few minutes to doodle something that's happened today: maybe a face you've seen, your lunch, an interesting building or whatever else takes your fancy.

`Use the space below to sketch and doodle`

Habit tracker   •   •   •   •   •   •   •   •   •

Mood tracker   ☀   🌙   Sleep   ☀   :   🌙   :

Today, I am greatful for .....

Date   /   /

Make them smile

You don't have to be a professional comedian to bring some fun, positivity and energy into other people's lives, especially those close to you. Make time to make someone smile today—help to brighten their day, even just for a short moment. It shows that you care. Have fun, be playful.

Write down your favourite jokes, or other things you've done or said that you know can cheer people up

Habit tracker   •   •   •   •   •   •   •   •   •

Mood tracker   ☀   ☾   Sleep   ☀   :   ☾   :

Today, I am greatful for .....

Dream easier

Without careful preparation, it's easy to let work stress creep up on us in the middle of the night. To sleep easy, before you leave work review your to-do list for the next day and carry out a breathing exercise or meditation. These will act as a barrier between your work and sleep.

Monitor your sleep disturbances and note where you can improve your barrier between work and sleep

Habit tracker   •   •   •   •   •   •   •   •   •

Mood tracker   ☀   ☾   Sleep   ☀   :   ☾   :

Today, I am greatful for .....

Odd socks, loud tops

Root around and find your brightest and silliest socks, dig out that Hawaiian shirt and why the heck not, bust out those bright trousers (maybe not all on the same day.) It might feel daunting, since these will naturally draw people's attention. But feeling self-conscious for just a short time isn't a bad thing: you'll start building confidence and resilience that you can draw on for more serious situations than socks.

List which garments you can try out: start small and work up your confidence from there

_____

_____

_____

_____

_____

_____

_____

_____

_____

_____

_____

_____

_____

_____

_____

_____

Habit tracker   •   •   •   •   •   •   •   •   •

Mood tracker   ☀   ☾   Sleep   ☀   :   ☾   :

Today, I am greatful for .....

Second office

Many people aren't built for flexible or co-working situations, let alone working nomadically. Some prefer the familiarity and safety of their own space. Even if it's just for half a day, try switching up your workspace. Take your laptop or notepad and move to a cosy chair in your kitchen, a coffee shop you've been meaning to try, your local library or somewhere else that takes your fancy and you'll find you work in new and different ways.

List potential new spaces that you can work in

Habit tracker   •   •   •   •   •   •   •   •   •

Mood tracker   ☀   🌙   Sleep   ☀   :   🌙   :

Today, I am greatful for .....

Inventory of unused ideas

When life whizzes past at top speed, it's hard to keep track of everything you've ever done or created. Set some time aside to go through your old work, dig out any ideas that didn't make the cut and look over any half-finished projects that you haven't thought about for a while. I guarantee you'll find some gold in there.

Write down any previously unused or unfinished ideas that you've rediscovered and want to explore further

Habit tracker   •   •   •   •   •   •   •   •   •

Mood tracker   ☀   ☾   Sleep   ☀   :   ☾   :

Today, I am greatful for .....

Frame it

We all have a few favourite spots where we feel at our most content. Some of those places are within walking distance, others might be thousands of miles away. Next time you find yourself in one of yours, take a photo of the location and repeat that process each time you visit. Compare the photos over time and see how that place changes with different light, shadows, times of the day and seasonal colours.

List and describe your favourite places. Why not sketch them?

Habit tracker   •   •   •   •   •   •   •   •   •

Mood tracker   ☀   🌙   Sleep   ☀   :   🌙   :

Today, I am greatful for .....

Notes and reflections

Burnout count

Sometimes we oscillate just an inch above our absolute rock bottom and we might not even know it. Have a think about how many times you've felt burned out in the past. Remind yourself how those situations felt and what led to them. There might have been more burnouts than you'd considered, and reflecting will help you spot the warning signs much sooner in future.

Reflect on what led to the times you've felt burned out before and how to avoid them in future

_____

_____

_____

_____

_____

_____

_____

_____

_____

_____

_____

_____

_____

_____

_____

_____

_____

_____

Habit tracker   •   •   •   •   •   •   •   •   •

Mood tracker   ☀   ☾   Sleep   ☀   :   ☾   :

Today, I am greatful for .....

_____

Something totally different

Long, drawn-out work projects can make you feel there's no end in sight and sap the life out of you, both in and outside of work. A great antidote is to set an hour aside at the end of your working day to start and finish something. That might be learning a new software technique, posting a project to your online portfolio or writing a page of your journal. Completing something different after a long day refreshes and wakes up your mind.

Think about and list the achievable, shorter-term tasks that you enjoy

Habit tracker   •   •   •   •   •   •   •   •   •

Mood tracker   ☀   🌙   Sleep   ☀   :   🌙   :

Today, I am greatful for .....

Structure your day

Only you know the times of day in which you're at your best. When can you focus the most? When do you usually feel more sluggish? Plan to do the tasks that require more concentration when you know you're sharpest, and the easier things for the times of day your mind tends to wander. That way, you make the most of your time.

`Note the times you're at your best and make`
`a structure for your day accordingly`

Habit tracker   •   •   •   •   •   •   •   •   •

Mood tracker   ☀   ☾   Sleep   ☀   :   ☾   :

Today, I am greatful for .....

Make a start and see where it takes you

No one sees happiness on a blank page. If you find yourself despairing in front of that dreaded empty piece of paper (or screen), start filling the space with a line, shape or a zig zag. Keep going. It feels meaningless, but it will make your mind come unstuck. Just make a small move. You have to start somewhere.

Draw a dot below, and start a line from there

Habit tracker

Mood tracker

Sleep

Today, I am greatful for .....

Bust a move, throw some shapes

Let music into your life. When you're battling those tough moments that you're struggling to snap out of, a good tune is a simple remedy—and it works. Dance like nobody's watching, get your heart rate up, get lost in music and the present moment. Air guitar encouraged.

List the songs that make you want to move

Habit tracker   •   •   •   •   •   •   •   •   •

Mood tracker   ☀   ☾   Sleep   ☀   :   ☾   :

Today, I am greatful for .....

Date   /   /

Take a step back

No one is capable of making sense of a situation while standing in the eye of the storm. You'll find that you can work so much better if you pause to step back from what you're making every so often. Take a moment to ponder, evaluate and take measure of what you've done so far. Reflect before you dive back in.

What were the last things that made more sense to you on reflection?

Habit tracker   •   •   •   •   •   •   •   •   •

Mood tracker   ☀   🌙   Sleep   ☀   :   🌙   :

Today, I am greatful for .....

Spectacles and moustaches

Allow yourself to be a child again by grabbing a copy of a newspaper or magazine and start drawing silly things on the faces: glasses, moustaches, devil horns and whatever else comes to mind. It's a great way of getting out of creative block through playfulness.

If there aren't any old publications around, start your silly doodles below

Habit tracker • • • • • • • • •

Mood tracker ☀ 🌙 Sleep ☀ : 🌙 :

Today, I am greatful for .....

Notes and reflections

Befriend the bad times

Some of the negative experiences around work we've been through in the past can feel impossible to forget. Remember, we all go through them. Recall how one such experience made you feel, and just sit with those uncomfortable feelings. Then focus on how you picked yourself back up. You'll learn how to cope better with bad situations instead of avoiding them.

Write down how you overcame a
recent negative experience

_____

_____

_____

_____

_____

_____

_____

_____

_____

_____

_____

_____

_____

_____

_____

_____

_____

_____

Habit tracker   •   •   •   •   •   •   •   •   •

Mood tracker   ☀   ☾   Sleep   ☀   :   ☾   :

Today, I am greatful for .....

_____

Be kind to yourself

Occasionally, creative work can feel like an endless vicious cycle of failing and failing again to make what we're striving for. Sometimes we fall just short of that frustratingly hard-to-cross finishing line. It's not you, it's the process. It's not meant to be easy. Remember to be kind to yourself.

`List the projects that you completed`
`which felt impossible along the way`

Habit tracker   •   •   •   •   •   •   •   •

Mood tracker   ☀   🌙   Sleep   ☀   :   🌙   :

Today, I am greatful for .....

Start small

Break big tasks into small chunks. You'll gradually find yourself making progress when working through manageable segments rather than being overwhelmed with the enormity of something. No one can move a mountain in one go. Over time, this technique will prove to be a useful skill in easily making sense of what first seems impossible.

What difficult task are you currently facing?

Where can you start?

_____

_____

_____

_____

_____

_____

_____

_____

_____

_____

_____

_____

_____

_____

_____

_____

Habit tracker   •   •   •   •   •   •   •   •   •

Mood tracker   ☀   🌙   Sleep   ☀   :   🌙   :

Today, I am greatful for .....

_____

New, old sounds

The world of classical music can feel impenetrable, but don't feel as though it's "not for you". If you've not heard much before, be assured it's a powerful tool for creativity. The intricate sonic layers and swirling melodies help you focus. Classical music can make the mind transcend and go to new places, and in doing so, make your work flow effortlessly.

List some classical music pieces, how they made you feel and their impact on your productivity

Habit tracker   •   •   •   •   •   •   •   •

Mood tracker   ☀   ☾   Sleep   ☀   :   ☾   :

Today, I am greatful for .....

Read and digest

Make time for mindful reading. Instead of skimming news articles or banal tweets, take a moment to read a chapter from a book and spend twice as much time thinking about what you've read afterwards. Fully digest the words, the rhythm, the plot. Consider what the chapter means, both in terms of the book's narrative and the world more generally.

Note any phrases, themes, characters, narrative devices or references you found interesting

Habit tracker   •   •   •   •   •   •   •   •   •

Mood tracker   ☀   ☾   Sleep   ☀   :   ☾   :

Today, I am greatful for .....

Find that deep stretch

Our bodies contain hundreds of muscles that work in unison every day. Some will naturally pull more weight than others, and we don't help them when we're hunched in front of a screen for hours on end. If you don't do so already, look up and try some yoga poses or stretches that focus on the muscles that need the most attention.

Note the muscles you feel need some TLC and the exercises you've learned that help

Habit tracker   •   •   •   •   •   •   •   •   •

Mood tracker   ☀   ☾   Sleep   ☀   :   ☾   :

Today, I am greatful for .....

Happy when it rains

We might complain when the weather turns wet and grey, but there's joy to be found in downpours. Find a shelter and spend five minutes just watching the world get bathed in fresh droplets of rain. Take in the scent of the air and the rhythmic drumming sounds as the water falls and hits the ground.

Describe the sound, smell and sensation
of rain next time it falls

_____

_____

_____

_____

_____

_____

_____

_____

_____

_____

_____

_____

_____

_____

Habit tracker   •   •   •   •   •   •   •   •   •

Mood tracker   ☀   🌙   Sleep   ☀   :   🌙   :

Today, I am greatful for .....

_____

Notes and reflections

Laugh out loud, then laugh a bit more

Great comedy is a peerless form of therapy. There's nothing like a deep belly laugh (or quiet giggle, if you happen to be on public transport) to shake you out of a funk. Rewatch your favourite shows and look into the comedians you love—it's likely they have a podcast, or clips and interviews you're yet to see. Comedy helps the world make a little more sense.

Jot down the comedians, podcasts and shows
you'd like to spend more time with

_____

_____

_____

_____

_____

_____

_____

_____

_____

_____

_____

_____

_____

_____

_____

_____

Habit tracker   •   •   •   •   •   •   •   •   •

Mood tracker   ☀   🌙   Sleep   ☀   :   🌙   :

Today, I am greatful for .....

Time off in sight

Many of us are terrible at taking time off, especially if we work for ourselves or run our own businesses. Look at your year ahead, book chunks of holiday in advance and make sure you actually take a break for a change. Trust me, your career won't collapse when you take a week or so off. Have something to look forward to.

Note down when you can take a week or so off and what you'll do with it

Habit tracker   •   •   •   •   •   •   •   •   •

Mood tracker   ☀   🌙   Sleep   ☀   :   🌙   :

Today, I am greatful for .....

pause

Mail over meetings

Work admin can be a stealthy thief of our time, especially if our schedules are run by other people. Endless meetings can make it impossible to actually sit down and get any work done, and these can often be dealt with by a quick email rather than a drawn-out event. It's ok to push back on requests when it means using your time more efficiently.

Tally up the time you've saved by choosing
to convert meetings to emails

_____

_____

_____

_____

_____

_____

_____

_____

_____

_____

_____

_____

_____

_____

_____

Habit tracker   •   •   •   •   •   •   •   •   •

Mood tracker   ☀   ☾   Sleep   ☀   :   ☾   :

Today, I am greatful for .....

Walk and talk

When you do need a physical meeting, sometimes the most productive ones are those in which you take yourself somewhere different. Try doing away with coffee shop tables and sterile boardrooms and take a meeting outdoors. The act of walking will help enhance your ideas and make you approach tasks in a new light.

List suitable, realistic places for
these kind of meetings

Habit tracker   •   •   •   •   •   •   •   •   •

Mood tracker   ☀   ☾   Sleep   ☀   :   ☾   :

Today, I am greatful for .....

Know your poison

Modern life is fuelled by billions of gallons of caffeine, alcoholic drinks and sugary sodas. These have a profound effect on how we feel and function—after all, what goes up has to come down. The short-term buzz from coffee, sugar or booze is likely to be followed by a cognitive and physical slump, whether in the immediate or long term—or both.

What will you cut down on or cut out?

Note it down with a start date

Habit tracker   •   •   •   •   •   •   •   •   •

Mood tracker   ☀   ☾   Sleep   ☀   :   ☾   :

Today, I am greatful for .....

Date   /   /

Be generous with praise

How often do you take the time to write a review of a good service that you've received? We're often far too busy living our lives to bother to tell someone they've been excellent. But even the shortest positive comment will spur someone on to keep going. It might only take one minute of your time, but it'll be a real boost for them.

What or who will you write a review for and why?

_____

_____

_____

_____

_____

_____

_____

_____

_____

_____

_____

_____

_____

_____

_____

Habit tracker   •   •   •   •   •   •   •   •   •

Mood tracker   ☀   ☾   Sleep   ☀   :   ☾   :

Today, I am greatful for .....

Think, don't fight

A tired mind can be quick to get irrationally aggressive and seek revenge for perceived wrongs. Instead, slow down, take a step back and collect your thoughts. Tune into how the situation is making you feel, both physically and emotionally. Accept everything that you're feeling rather than fighting it. Take a few deep, long breaths before deciding what to do. Understanding a situation from all sides helps to diffuse anger, let in compassion and maintain calm.

Describe a recent instance when you got upset and how you managed to calm down

Habit tracker   •   •   •   •   •   •   •   •   •

Mood tracker   ☀   ☾   Sleep   ☀   :   ☾   :

Today, I am greatful for .....

Notes and reflections

Notes and reflections

Notes and reflections

breathe

When anxiety or stress overwhelm us, it's easy for our minds to plunge down to even darker depths. That freefall can seem very real and frighteningly endless if we don't intervene. At times like that, the way to navigate back to safety is through our breath.

If you've followed this journal from the start, you'll have put into practice the suggestions to help you pause. In this section, you'll be adding mindful breathing to those pauses and using the two concepts in conjunction with one another. The ability to tune in to your own breath and connect it to your body will enable you to find meaningful experiences throughout your day, and to do so in any number of situations.

The prompts in this chapter are designed to help you find peace and clarity through carefully observing each present moment and your own thoughts. They look at bringing focus to our inner worlds, and learning to become non-judgemental in our views of past negative experiences. The ability to take time to breathe is an innate tool that can rescue us from immediate panic and help us move forward.

Time to breathe

It's easy to make excuses that you don't have the time to make changes, but we all have a spare couple of minutes to tune into our breath at least once a day. You can be sitting at your desk, standing in a queue or walking to the shops; just take a few moments to notice your breathing. It's a great anchor to bring us right into the present. Factor this into your routine and soon it will be a natural and normal daily habit.

Tune into your breath once a day

Habit tracker   •   •   •   •   •   •   •   •   •

Mood tracker   ☀   ☾   Sleep   ☀   :   ☾   :

Today, I am greatful for .....

Breathe into your body

Try this exercise: inhale deeply and connect your breathing with different parts of your body. Starting with your feet and slowly moving upward, breathe in and imagine the air flowing to different parts of your body, observing the sensations you feel as you go. Then exhale fully and observe how each part feels and moves as the breath leaves the body. You'll notice how the breath and the body work in perfect harmony. Focus on the sensation of deep, controlled breathing. These sensations will be a central part of your new, calmer life.

Record the new sensations you feel

Habit tracker • • • • • • • • •

Mood tracker ☀ ☾ Sleep ☀ : ☾ :

Today, I am greatful for .....

Tune into your body

Try the "body scan": starting with the top of your head and travelling slowly down to your feet, pay attention to each and every sensation you find in your body. Don't judge what you find or don't find: sometimes you'll notice tingling, sometimes different temperatures, maybe soreness or lightness, while with some areas you don't notice anything. Just accept everything you find. End with feeling the contact of your body with your seat, or your feet with the floor. The body is another great anchor to draw our minds right into the present moment and break mental chatter.

Record how this exercise feels across different days as you practice

Download an audio version of this meditation - see page 192

Habit tracker   •   •   •   •   •   •   •   •   •

Mood tracker   ☀   ☽   Sleep   ☀   :   ☽   :

Today, I am greatful for .....

Ten minutes early

Set your alarm ten minutes earlier than you normally do. Take those ten minutes to do some breathing exercises before you start your day. Lie back and focus on your breathing. Feel yourself sinking into your bed as you breathe. You'll feel like you get to rest a bit longer without running late and feel more energised for the day ahead.

Note down your progress in managing this
and the changes you've seen as a result

Habit tracker •   •   •   •   •   •   •   •   •

Mood tracker   ☀   ☾   Sleep   ☀   :   ☾   :

Today, I am greatful for .....

You are not your thoughts

From time to time some dark or troublesome thoughts might cross our mind. Don't let them define you—they are just thoughts. Creative minds don't only conjure up good things, they can conjure up dark clouds too. However, like clouds in the sky, these thoughts will pass if you let them go. It can help to spend some time watching our thoughts as they come and go and to label them. For example, "here's a thought about money worries, there's a thought about my deadline, there's a thought about lunch." Soon you'll start seeing them from a distance as opposed to identifying yourself with them.

Label your thoughts by writing them down

Habit tracker   •   •   •   •   •   •   •   •   •

Mood tracker   ☀   🌙   Sleep   ☀   :   🌙   :

Today, I am greatful for .....

We're still here

When you wake up, remind yourself of what lies ahead for the day. Celebrate the fact that you get to see another day and revel in all the things you have achieved in previous ones. Chase the sunrise and remind yourself that you can take on the world again.

Make a note of what you're grateful for each day

Habit tracker   •   •   •   •   •   •   •   •

Mood tracker   ☀   🌙   Sleep   ☀   :   🌙   :

Today, I am greatful for .....

Get out

Stop eating lunch at your desk. As difficult as it might seem, take some time away from your computer. Leave the office, or your house if you work from home, and spend at least ten minutes outside. Get some fresh air, take a walk around the block. You'll be amazed at how much better you'll feel when you come back.

Record how lunchtime fresh air impacts
your afternoons over time

Habit tracker   •   •   •   •   •   •   •   •   •

Mood tracker   ☀   🌙   Sleep   ☀   :   🌙   :

Today, I am greatful for .....

Notes and reflections

Turn off the autopilot

It's easy for our days to blend into a homogenous blur. When our brains realise that we're doing something we've done before, it decides to fill in the blanks. You can avoid this by making small changes each day. Take a new route to work, or get something different for lunch. The more variation to your days, the better.

`Plan the change you're going to make each day`

Habit tracker   •   •   •   •   •   •   •   •   •

Mood tracker   ☀   🌙   Sleep   ☀   :   🌙   :

Today, I am greatful for .....

Walking meditation

Most of us don't walk for fun, but to get somewhere. Often you'll find that you can't really remember anything about your route. Our minds are filled with thoughts about how hectic life and work is. Take a walk, pay attention and use your senses. Look at the sky and the colours, smell the air, touch the plants. Forget about the everyday details and breathe easily for a while.

`Jot down observations from your walks`

Habit tracker   •   •   •   •   •   •   •   •   •

Mood tracker   ☀   ☽   Sleep   ☀   :   ☽   :

Today, I am greatful for .....

Netflix and (actually) chill

We've all been there: you put on a movie, take out your phone, check your social media and email. Soon the film's over and you have no idea what it was actually about. Next time you watch a movie leave your phone in the other room or turn it off. Hopefully, you'll finally be fully absorbed in the movie narrative.

List your favourite movie quotes,
plot twists, characters and scenes

Habit tracker   •   •   •   •   •   •   •   •   •

Mood tracker   ☀   🌙   Sleep   ☀   :   🌙   :

Today, I am greatful for .....

You're more than good enough

It often feels like everyone else is more wealthy, talented or successful than you are. It's easy to let thoughts like that run away with us, but that never ends well. You're great at what you do and you're more than good enough. Never forget that.

Create a daily self-affirmation and write it down.

Eg. "I am good enough"

Habit tracker   •   •   •   •   •   •   •   •   •

Mood tracker   ☀   ☾   Sleep   ☀   :   ☾   :

Today, I am greatful for .....

You're not alone

As soon as you start to panic, it becomes increasingly difficult to see the bigger picture and take in everything that's going on. In the moments before we determine what's actually wrong—why we're panicking at all—we likely can't see or admit that there's a problem. At times like that it can feel as though our problem is unique. It isn't: you're never the only one.

Share your feelings with a friend or confidante
and note how it made you feel

Habit tracker   •   •   •   •   •   •   •   •   •

Mood tracker   ☀   🌙   Sleep   ☀   :   🌙   :

Today, I am greatful for .....

Comfort in sound

Make a playlist of your favourite songs and keep it at the ready when you need a moment of calm. Play one of the songs and listen to it carefully. You might pick up something that you've never noticed before: that guitar solo you've heard a million times before might sound even better if you listen to every last note.

Listen to a favourite song as if it's the first time

Habit tracker   •   •   •   •   •   •   •   •   •

Mood tracker   ☀   ☾   Sleep   ☀   :   ☾   :

Today, I am greatful for .....

One thing at the time

Stop trying to be the master multi-tasker. Your mind is a bit like a web browser: we often have too many tabs open, and it's important to close the unnecessary ones to help focus on one thing at a time. Work to complete each task rather than starting something new halfway through.

Celebrate and note when you complete a task without interrupting it by starting another

Habit tracker   •   •   •   •   •   •   •   •   •

Mood tracker   ☀   ☾   Sleep   ☀   :   ☾   :

Today, I am greatful for .....

Notes and reflections

No more horror movies

Our worries can manifest in ways that make us see nothing but the worst case scenarios. It's called catastrophising: our minds create entire scenes showcasing the horrors that might lay ahead. However, choosing to be calm and rational allows us to see that these horrors are just fictional products of our minds running away with us. When we stop to ask: "is this happening now?" the answer is usually "no", and we can bring ourselves back into the present.

Next time you're fearing a catastrophe, stop and ask: is it happening now?

Habit tracker   •   •   •   •   •   •   •   •   •

Mood tracker   ☀   🌙   Sleep   ☀   :   🌙   :

Today, I am greatful for .....

Amazing grace

Friendly people are generous with kind words and compliments. Accept these compliments graciously and say thank you, don't just dismiss them or brush them off. Be grateful whenever you can. It'll feel great to return the generosity that's been offered to you.

Note each time you manage to say "thank you"
and accept compliments graciously

Habit tracker   •   •   •   •   •   •   •   •   •

Mood tracker   ☀   ☾   Sleep   ☀   :   ☾   :

Today, I am greatful for .....

Smile on the inside

The world can be a pretty silly place if you look carefully enough for moments of playfulness. There's always something to smile about or a joke to be found somewhere if you dig a little deeper. Even if that thing which makes you chuckle is only funny to you, it's ok to smile about it. You won't look crazy—and who cares if anyone else thinks you do?

Describe the moments that
made you smile each day

Habit tracker   •   •   •   •   •   •   •   •   •

Mood tracker   ☀   🌙   Sleep   ☀   :   🌙   :

Today, I am greatful for .....

The price of happiness

Working towards happiness takes time and effort. It can often feel as though the world is working against us—be assured that it isn't. Keep going and working through the obstacles that cross your path. Notice all the things that align and help when you're putting the work in.

Reflect on the positive actions that
have led you to happiness before

Habit tracker   •   •   •   •   •   •   •   •   •

Mood tracker   ☀   ☾   Sleep   ☀   :   ☾   :

Today, I am greatful for .....

Shutdown signals

Identify a time and place to truly shut down your mind after the working day. Train yourself to recognise that moment and location as a signal to switch off. Maybe it's the commute home, a gym session, walking your dog or just finding a spot at home to focus on making the transition out of work mode.

Write down how you feel these actions help you let go of work stress

Habit tracker   •   •   •   •   •   •   •   •   •

Mood tracker   ☀   🌙   Sleep   ☀   :   🌙   :

Today, I am greatful for .....

Tune in to silence

Once your working day is over, learn to spend time alone with your thoughts. Those moments of reflection are a luxury you should afford yourself every single day. Make time to process your thoughts in silence, even if only for a few minutes.

Turn off all devices and be alone
with yourself once a day

_____

_____

_____

_____

_____

_____

_____

_____

_____

_____

_____

_____

_____

_____

_____

_____

_____

Habit tracker   •   •   •   •   •   •   •   •   •

Mood tracker   ☀   ☾   Sleep   ☀   :   ☾   :

Today, I am greatful for .....

You're free

Always remember that you are independent and have free will. Think about the things that make you feel free and in charge of your present, past and future. Despite the problems of the modern world, we have more opportunities and chances to learn than we ever have. We live in arguably the most free society in history. Cherish that fact.

Make a list of the things you're free to do,
and what makes you feel free

_____

_____

_____

_____

_____

_____

_____

_____

_____

_____

_____

_____

_____

_____

_____

_____

Habit tracker   •   •   •   •   •   •   •   •   •

Mood tracker   ☀   🌙   Sleep   ☀   :   🌙   :

Today, I am greatful for .....

_____

Notes and reflections

Bedtime routine

It can feel like a battle to get eight hours sleep each night with everything else going on in our lives. It's all too easy to build up a sleep deficit, even over a short period of time. Define your bedtime and make sure you stick with it, just like you do with your morning alarm.

Outline a routine you can stick to that helps prepare for a regular sleep time

Habit tracker   •   •   •   •   •   •   •   •   •

Mood tracker   ☀   ☾   Sleep   ☀   :   ☾   :

Today, I am greatful for .....

Nap time

If you work from home, make time to sneak in an afternoon nap. Getting just 15 minutes or so of shut-eye can be a real boost and perk you up on a dreary, tiring day. Set a timer, experiment with various nap-lengths and you might see why the concept of a siesta is one that many people can't live without.

Note how often you nap and how long for, then how it makes you feel

Habit tracker   •   •   •   •   •   •   •   •   •

Mood tracker   ☀   🌙   Sleep   ☀   :   🌙   :

Today, I am greatful for .....

Accept your place in the crowd

When you find yourself stuck in a queue and you're running late, don't blame the people in front of you. You aren't just stuck in traffic, you're part of it. These things are realities we have to accept. Take a deep breath and work through a breathing exercise. In time, these moments will become less stressful and you'll build more resilience to deal with them.

Next time you have to get somewhere, revise your plan
to factor in anything that might hold you up

Habit tracker   •   •   •   •   •   •   •   •   •

Mood tracker   ☀   🌙   Sleep   ☀   :   🌙   :

Today, I am greatful for .....

Watch your levels

Much like the frog in a pot of boiling water doesn't notice the temperature until it's too late, it can be difficult for us to sense our stress levels rising. Often we need other people to let us know that we're not acting like ourselves. Being honest about our mental state and our stress levels is crucial in helping us deal with them.

Ask those around you how they see
your stress levels and take note

Habit tracker   •   •   •   •   •   •   •   •   •

Mood tracker   ☀   🌙   Sleep   ☀   :   🌙   :

Today, I am greatful for .....

Reality check

It's easy to feel overwhelmed and confused in stressful situations, especially if you're already feeling fragile. Stop, take a deep breath and look around to take stock of the real situation. How far are you really in danger? What's a real threat, and what's your mind just running away with you? Often you'll find that your mind is just used to catastrophising, and you need to reassure it.

Ask yourself what danger you're in

Habit tracker   •   •   •   •   •   •   •   •   •

Mood tracker   ☀   ☾   Sleep   ☀   :   ☾   :

Today, I am greatful for .....

Ambition anxiety

Many of us have big career ambitions—maybe you want to use your creativity to start amazing brands or launch groundbreaking startups. It's never going to end well if you try to do everything, right this second—as tempting as it might be. Don't rush: good things take time. Think about your journey, the steps along the way and plan a (realistic) launch date.

Transfer any racing thoughts into a list
of planned actions here

Habit tracker   •   •   •   •   •   •   •   •   •

Mood tracker   ☀   ☾   Sleep   ☀   :   ☾   :

Today, I am greatful for .....

Unrealistic workload

Despite the technologies at our fingertips, we still tend to work overtime far too often. We cram in as much extra work as we can, even though no one expects us to. As a result we sabotage ourselves and our time by trying to do the impossible. Be realistic about what you need to do today and what can wait.

Revise your to-do list into two manageable lists, one for today and one for less urgent tasks

Habit tracker   •   •   •   •   •   •   •   •   •

Mood tracker   ☀   🌙   Sleep   ☀   :   🌙   :

Today, I am greatful for .....

Notes and reflections

Bird's eye view

There are two sides to every story but we tend to only see one—ours. It's easy to only view the world solely through the lens of our own thoughts and expectations. Instead, try viewing the world like a drone looking down. That way you can see what the situation really is before you make a judgement.

Note how others might view a situation you're struggling with and compare it to your own outlook

Habit tracker   •   •   •   •   •   •   •   •   •

Mood tracker   ☀   🌙   Sleep   ☀   :   🌙   :

Today, I am greatful for .....

Know your impact

Our stress and anxiety can have a profound effect on the people around us. By using breathing techniques and mindfulness, we can calm the frenetic pace of our mind and slow down our heart rate. Be present and observant, and realise the calming effect this will have on others in turn.

Think about potentially stressful situations
coming up and pre-empt them here

Habit tracker   •   •   •   •   •   •   •   •   •

Mood tracker   ☀   🌙   Sleep   ☀   :   🌙   :

Today, I am greatful for .....

Leave the digital world at the door

A mind that's scattered in numerous directions can derail anyone's train of thought when trying to work. For some reason we feel the need to look up random facts on Wikipedia, check the news or look at social media. If you feel unable to resist such temptations, try putting a time lock on your browser or deleting certain apps from your phone.

Record the temptations to procrastinate
that you managed to avoid today

Habit tracker   •   •   •   •   •   •   •   •   •

Mood tracker   ☀   🌙   Sleep   ☀   :   🌙   :

Today, I am greatful for .....

Why am I here?

How many people are able to answer that question off the top of their head? Sure, life would feel a lot easier if we knew our true purpose. However, no one does. Accept uncertainty. Instead of trying to find the answer to the impossible, enjoy the excitement of trying to discover your personal purpose and how it can help others.

Describe what you feel has been/is your purpose at this stage of your life

_____

_____

_____

_____

_____

_____

_____

_____

_____

_____

_____

_____

_____

_____

_____

_____

_____

Habit tracker   •   •   •   •   •   •   •   •   •

Mood tracker   ☀   🌙   Sleep   ☀   :   🌙   :

Today, I am greatful for .....

The big day ahead

All significant occasions will make people feel naturally apprehensive. A big presentation, project hand-in or personal review can make you understandably nervous. Run through the task ahead and prepare for all possible outcomes.

Write down the things you usually find yourself worrying about and score them from 1–5 (1 meaning low-level worry, 5 being highest level of panic)

Habit tracker   •   •   •   •   •   •   •   •   •

Mood tracker   ☀   🌙   Sleep   ☀   :   🌙   :

Today, I am greatful for .....

Clean hands, clear mind

Those hand-washing guidance posters we see everywhere aren't just handy for hygiene—they're a great tool for mindfulness. Instead of singing Happy Birthday twice to make sure you're washing for 20 seconds, use each step as a grounding to stay present in the moment, taking in every movement and each tiny part of skin as you scrub.

Run your mind through every movement as you follow the instructions

---

Habit tracker   •   •   •   •   •   •   •   •   •

Mood tracker   ☀   ☾   Sleep   ☀   :   ☾   :

Today, I am greatful for .....

No agenda

To be completely present, why not see how you spend a day off without planning anything in advance? From the moment you wake up, allow yourself to just be, and see what you do from moment to moment. You might surprise yourself with what transpires as you allow this level of spontaneity and flow. Trust in the moment, and trust yourself.

Take a day off without planning
anything in advance

Habit tracker   •   •   •   •   •   •   •   •   •

Mood tracker   ☀   🌙   Sleep   ☀   :   🌙   :

Today, I am greatful for .....

Notes and reflections

Notes and reflections

Notes and reflections

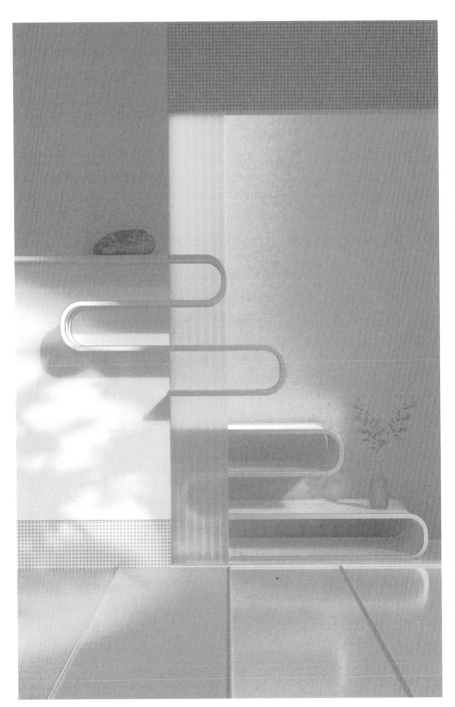

grow

It's easy to get lost on our life and career journeys if we lack direction. Without a clearly signposted destination, it's easy to aimlessly meander through the nine-to-five and feel like we've got little to show for it afterwards.

This third set of prompts aims to help you draw yourself a map that enables you to make sense of the here and now in order to make sense of the future. Start by considering where you are at the moment, and think about the aspects you're happy with and those which need improvement. Then plan how you can grow in your career, set future goals and envision how you can celebrate them. Think about what will make you happiest.

These pages also look to help you become more resilient and more able to cope with what the world throws at you, both personally and professionally. Whether you're flexing your creative muscles to earn a living or not, all job roles come with their own set of challenges. It's easy to feel like everyone has it easier than us—they don't. It's up to you to keep your own career moving forward: you're in charge of taking yourself to the next step and allowing yourself time to grow.

Yesterday, today and forever

Renew your commitment to your chosen creative field and career journey. This is the path that you've chosen. To do well in your work—and enjoy it—you need to maintain an unshakeable belief that it's right for you. It won't always be plain sailing, but you got this far and you can, and will, continue to shine.

Note how long you've been in your chosen field and why you know it's right for you

Habit tracker   •   •   •   •   •   •   •   •   •

Mood tracker   ☀   ☾   Sleep   ☀   :   ☾   :

Today, I am greatful for .....

Friendly fire

Let's be honest: when you show your work to friends and family, more often than not you're just seeking approval and praise. But sometimes, people close to you will volunteer feedback you didn't ask for. They don't want to criticise you or make you unhappy, they just care. Learn to accept and appreciate their positive intentions.

Jot down any recent comments
you found to be helpful

Habit tracker   •   •   •   •   •   •   •   •   •

Mood tracker   ☀   ☾   Sleep   ☀   :   ☾   :

Today, I am greatful for .....

Own your motivation

Define your personal creative philosophy. What gets you up in the morning? What gives you a kick? Why do you keep persevering, even when things feel impossible? What drives you time and time again? Who benefits from your creativity?

Describe what creativity means to you

Habit tracker   •   •   •   •   •   •   •   •   •

Mood tracker   ☀   🌙   Sleep   ☀   :   🌙   :

Today, I am greatful for .....

Celebrate good times

Successes both big and small are always worth celebrating. Enjoy the moment, then make a note of what went well: why and how you won a project, delivered a great piece of work or succeeded in something despite difficult odds. Taking stock when things go well means you're more likely to repeat those successes.

`List your recent wins and`
`what made them possible`

_____

_____

_____

_____

_____

_____

_____

_____

_____

_____

_____

_____

_____

_____

_____

_____

_____

_____

_____

| Habit tracker | ● | ● | ● | ● | ● | ● | ● | ● | ● |

| Mood tracker | ☀ | | 🌙 | | Sleep | ☀ | : | 🌙 | : |

Today, I am greatful for .....

Celebrate bad times, too

Just as you should celebrate your victories, embrace the times when things didn't go to plan, too. No one wins every time. Failure is part of growing and learning, as well as building resilience for when things are tough in future. Any insights you can spot around what went wrong are immeasurably helpful, and turn your failures into small successes next time.

List your recent failures and what you've
learned to avoid repeating those mistakes

Habit tracker   •   •   •   •   •   •   •   •   •

Mood tracker   ☀   ☾   Sleep   ☀   :   ☾   :

Today, I am greatful for .....

What does success look like?

Define your creative business's battle plan and list its previous victories. Making an inventory of those will help you plan where to go next. Do you want to expand the business and employ hundreds of staff, or stay small but ambitious and agile? Want to make millions? What sort of work environment makes you happiest? What does success look like to you?

List what you want to achieve and describe
what success looks like to you

Habit tracker   •   •   •   •   •   •   •   •   •

Mood tracker   ☀   ☾   Sleep   ☀   :   ☾   :

Today, I am greatful for .....

Dream work, dream clients

The grass isn't always greener: if you're actively making creative work, you're already achieving something that many find impossible. People are putting their trust and money into your work when they hire you, so take a moment to appreciate that fact. Dream clients are the ones you already have.

List your favourite clients
and projects

Habit tracker   •   •   •   •   •   •   •   •   •

Mood tracker   ☀   🌙   Sleep   ☀   :   🌙   :

Today, I am greatful for .....

Notes and reflections

Small budget? No problem

Every business has to start somewhere. The magic of small brands is in seeing them bear fruit down the line. When you get the chance to work with new companies and startups, it's your creativity and ideas that can be the vehicle to make them the best they can be.

List all the clients who started small and grew to be your top billers over time

Habit tracker   •   •   •   •   •   •   •   •   •

Mood tracker   ☀   🌙   Sleep   ☀   :   🌙   :

Today, I am greatful for .....

Look out for tomorrow

Always have one eye looking to the future, especially when everything is rosy today. While it's often hard to even consider glancing away from your current workload, it's important to set aside part of the day for future plans. A single email, call or chance to make a new connection (your goal is for one of these each day) could be the thing that gets you where you want to go next.

Make a list of actions and people to
contact you can achieve this week

Habit tracker   •   •   •   •   •   •   •   •   •

Mood tracker   ☀   ☾   Sleep   ☀   :   ☾   :

Today, I am greatful for .....

Don't be shy

We've never had as many opportunities to connect with people, so use them. Contact your idol, find a mentor whose work you admire, or reach out to your favourite musician or artist and suggest a collaboration. Don't just wait for things to come to you—actively try to make them happen.

List the people or companies you aim to
contact and when/how you'll do it

Habit tracker •   •   •   •   •   •   •   •   •

Mood tracker ☀   🌙   Sleep   ☀   :   🌙   :

Today, I am greatful for .....

In it together

Spare a minute to contact a peer working in your field and give them a sincere compliment on their work. It shows your confidence and kindness when you celebrate other people's achievements. Whatever industry you work in, we're all just people trying to make things work. Make allies, not enemies.

List the names of people you admire and
why they inspire you to do better work

Habit tracker   •   •   •   •   •   •   •   •

Mood tracker   ☀   ☾   Sleep   ☀   :   ☾   :

Today, I am greatful for .....

Show up and speak up

The world would be a very boring place if it didn't contain so many incredibly talented introverts. You might happen to be one of them. While it might seem daunting, start using your voice to talk about your experiences, work, processes and creative thinking. Speaking in front of people or presenting your work might seem scary, but your confidence will grow with every sentence.

Plan a verbal review for a piece of your work
to make its rationale even stronger

Habit tracker   •   •   •   •   •   •   •   •   •

Mood tracker   ☀   🌙   Sleep   ☀   :   🌙   :

Today, I am greatful for .....

This time last year

Look over the body of work you've created over the past 12 months. There's every chance you barely remember what you did a few weeks ago, let alone a year ago. Reflect on how far you've come, the progress you've made and celebrate what you've managed to achieve.

What were the highlights and low points
of the past 12 months?

_____

_____

_____

_____

_____

_____

_____

_____

_____

_____

_____

_____

_____

_____

_____

_____

Habit tracker   •   •   •   •   •   •   •   •   •

Mood tracker   ☀   🌙   Sleep   ☀   :   🌙   :

Today, I am greatful for .....

Explore the landscape

Once you've identified the kind of clients or markets you want to work with, learn all you can about them. Read up, chat to people working in those industries, learn the landscape inside out and start to speak the same language. Look out for the challenges these sort of clients face—you might be just the person to solve them.

List all sources that can help you collect the knowledge you need

Habit tracker   •   •   •   •   •   •   •   •   •

Mood tracker   ☀   ☾   Sleep   ☀   :   ☾   :

Today, I am greatful for .....

Notes and reflections

Workload dissonance

A sense of dissatisfaction with how much work you do (or don't) have right now is pretty universal. Everyone panics when things get quieter and wishes they had just a few more projects on. When things are manic, you're begging for the world to cut you some slack. It's almost impossible to find a happy medium, you just have to learn to accept that.

Review your current workload and remind yourself
that it's not too large, or too small

Habit tracker   •   •   •   •   •   •   •   •   •

Mood tracker   ☀   🌙   Sleep   ☀   :   🌙   :

Today, I am greatful for .....

Silence is (occasionally) golden

Cherish the quieter times. Being busy is great in that it keeps you on your toes, but when things slow down for a few days—even weeks—your brain and business get a well-earned chance to recharge. Use those times to catch up on admin, work on personal projects and plan for the future. Those things are vital for growth and keep you sane.

Write down when you'll less busy and how
you can use that time to grow

Habit tracker   •   •   •   •   •   •   •   •   •

Mood tracker   ☀   🌙   Sleep   ☀   :   🌙   :

Today, I am greatful for .....

Find your niche

Become the go-to person for your skills and expertise in a particular area. You already have a unique way of thinking and applying your creativity, so use it to become the best in whatever niche you're carving out. Stay true to yourself and success will follow.

Write down the area(s) in which you have unique skills and knowledge

_____

_____

_____

_____

_____

_____

_____

_____

_____

_____

_____

_____

_____

_____

_____

_____

_____

Habit tracker   •   •   •   •   •   •   •   •   •

Mood tracker   ☀   ☾   Sleep   ☀   :   ☾   :

Today, I am greatful for .....

Your creative arsenal

Take stock of what you've mastered so far. List your skills, the sort of work you can do with your eyes closed, the things that you can do that few others can and the unique things about your creative approach. Write them all down: once you start thinking about them, there's likely a lot more there than you realise.

What are your strongest skills and why?

_____

_____

_____

_____

_____

_____

_____

_____

_____

_____

_____

_____

_____

_____

_____

Habit tracker   •   •   •   •   •   •   •   •   •

Mood tracker   ☀   🌙   Sleep   ☀   :   🌙   :

Today, I am greatful for .....

What future-you can do

Identify what might hold you back from fulfilling your future ambitions. Jot down the skills you need to gain or work on which will help you get to where you want to be. These could be mastering job or funding applications, learning new software, improving certain life skills or overcoming a fear of public speaking. Start with one of them and gradually work through the list.

List your ambitions along with the skills
you need to learn to achieve them

Habit tracker   •   •   •   •   •   •   •   •   •

Mood tracker   ☀   🌙   Sleep   ☀   :   🌙   :

Today, I am greatful for .....

New skills, new you

Plan for continuous learning: think about the new skills that might benefit you or the ones you have already that you want to improve. Some of these won't be easy, and new skills take time to master, but it'll be worth the effort if you stick with your plan. Set time aside daily, weekly or monthly to get started. Even a few minutes a day can really add up.

Write down when and where you will have time to learn

Habit tracker   •   •   •   •   •   •   •   •   •

Mood tracker   ☀   🌙   Sleep   ☀   :   🌙   :

Today, I am greatful for .....

Opportunities will knock

Don't feel as though you have to leap to say yes to every single commission you're offered. Equally, don't panic if you're faced with a dry spell. More opportunities are around the corner, and they might just be better ones. Do away with desperation: you'll feel happier and more liberated if you shake the feeling that you "need" every single job that you're offered.

Remind yourself of your good and bad decisions so far when it comes to accepting projects

Habit tracker   •   •   •   •   •   •   •   •   •

Mood tracker   ☀   ☾   Sleep   ☀   :   ☾   :

Today, I am greatful for .....

Notes and reflections

Thanks but no thanks

Saying no to things that you're concerned might not be good for you is empowering. It's all too easy to feel obliged to agree to projects that promise great opportunities but which end up wasting your time and energy. Today's decisions always have an impact on what happens tomorrow.

Write down the offers you've declined previously and why

Habit tracker   •   •   •   •   •   •   •   •   •

Mood tracker   ☀   ☾   Sleep   ☀   :   ☾   :

Today, I am greatful for .....

Facing fears

An inability to co-exist with our fears can stand in the way of what we want to achieve. No one is fear-free, we just have to learn to put them in their place and accept them as part of life. Tackling our fears head on will gradually decrease their intensity, a little like exercising a muscle.

Write down your fears and the day you
plan to start facing them

Habit tracker   •   •   •   •   •   •   •   •   •

Mood tracker   ☀   ☾   Sleep   ☀   :   ☾   :

Today, I am greatful for .....

The final sprint

Short projects can be intense and fun. Longer projects, however, take a more indepth and immersive approach that can easily drain you if they drag on and on. When you're flagging, just remember to keep going and that the end is in sight. The long game will feel much more manageable if you list the outstanding tasks and start ticking them off as you go.

Note the outstanding tasks for a large project and split them into manageable daily lists

Habit tracker

Mood tracker   ☀   🌙   Sleep   ☀   :   🌙   :

Today, I am greatful for .....

You can't please everyone

You can't always choose an audience. What you make may well travel far beyond those you'd hoped it would appeal to. People won't always like what you do, and that's ok. Once something's out in the world it's beyond your control. Remind yourself that some things aren't your cup of tea, either.

Note down the work or people you've
stopped to admire this week

Habit tracker   •   •   •   •   •   •   •   •   •

Mood tracker   ☀   🌙   Sleep .   ☀   :   🌙   :

Today, I am greatful for .....

Date / /

Quality time

We all have different methods when it comes to time management, and what's right for one person might be a nightmare for another. Evaluate whether or not your current time management tool is working as well as it could do. Test out different ways of managing your time, both analogue and digital, to find the one that's most effective for your life and process.

List the pros and cons of your current approach and ask others for their time-management suggestions

Habit tracker

Mood tracker   ☀   🌙   Sleep   ☀   :   🌙   :

Today, I am greatful for .....

Where does the day go?

Even the days planned with military precision can suddenly draw to a close and leave you feeling as though you've barely scratched the surface of what you wanted to achieve. When there's a lot on your plate, remind yourself of what you did do, rather than what you didn't. It'll be more than you realise.

Note what you've managed to tick off from
your to-do list at the end of each day

Habit tracker   •   •   •   •   •   •   •   •   •

Mood tracker   ☀   ☾   Sleep   ☀   :   ☾   :

Today, I am greatful for .....

Shit happens

Make peace with discomfort. Stuff breaks, people let you down, invoices get paid late. Life gets in the way of work, work gets in the way of life. Nobody's happy all the time, and it's unhelpful to expect ourselves to be. Make peace with the fact there'll be more bumps in the road ahead of you, and ahead of everyone else, too.

Write down what might go wrong today or this week in order to plan ahead for it

Habit tracker   •   •   •   •   •   •   •   •   •

Mood tracker   ☀   🌙   Sleep   ☀   :   🌙   :

Today, I am greatful for .....

Notes and reflections

Stay hungry for knowledge

Those who hunger for knowledge and keep learning are those who have richer outlooks. There's never an excuse not to learn: think about what you're interested in and dig deeper by visiting online galleries and research archives, and taking part in digital workshops. You'll develop more rounded views when it comes to both life and creative work.

If you don't plan it, it won't happen. Make a list of areas and topics of interest for you

Habit tracker   •   •   •   •   •   •   •   •   •

Mood tracker   ☀   ☾   Sleep   ☀   :   ☾   :

Today, I am greatful for .....

Learn to love deadlines

The excitement of starting a new project can quickly dwindle into procrastination. It's never good to rush things, but where possible try to work ahead of schedule. That way, you finish earlier, get paid earlier (hopefully) and have more time built in for anything that might go wrong at the final hurdle. It's far less stressful than last minute panicking.

Revise your project timelines to see what you might be able to deliver early

Habit tracker   •   •   •   •   •   •   •   •   •

Mood tracker   ☀   ☾   Sleep   ☀   :   ☾   :

Today, I am greatful for .....

Keep on questioning

It's great to be curious—sometimes even nosey—if it means taking interest in other people's processes and continually learning. Take a peek behind the scenes to find out how those you admire really go about what they do. Ask them everything you can ("why, what, where, when, how" is a good place to start) about their thought processes, working days and go to-tricks.

Note who you want to contact and what questions you want to ask them

Habit tracker   •   •   •   •   •   •   •   •   •

Mood tracker   ☀   ☾   Sleep   ☀   :   ☾   :

Today, I am greatful for .....

Pick their brains, and pass it on

Ask the people you look up to and whose work you admire for book or podcast recommendations that will enrich your knowledge of your craft. With so much free content out there, it's daft not to tap into it and benefit from it on both personal and creative levels. Pass on those recommendations to others and help them grow, too.

List the recommendations you've solicited from people here

Habit tracker   •   •   •   •   •   •   •   •   •

Mood tracker   ☀   ☾   Sleep   ☀   :   ☾   :

Today, I am greatful for .....

Write your story

Draft the first paragraph of your monograph. How do you see your body of work, and how do you think others see it? We all have a story to tell, and our creativity is a huge part of what makes up the narrative and how it's told. What do you want others to know about your work, and what's the best way you can communicate it?

Draft a paragraph and
review it each week

Habit tracker   •   •   •   •   •   •   •   •   •

Mood tracker   ☀   ☾   Sleep   ☀   :   ☾   :

Today, I am greatful for .....

You're already there

A great mental exercise for motivation is to imagine that you've already achieved your desired outcome, and just sit with how it makes you feel. Let those positive feelings and sensations dance around in your awareness, and enjoy the feeling. Then make sure you do something every day to make this a reality, no matter how small or large the action is.

Imagine you've already got what you wanted and sit with that feeling

Habit tracker   •   •   •   •   •   •   •   •   •

Mood tracker   ☀   🌙   Sleep   ☀   :   🌙   :

Today, I am greatful for .....

Thank you notes

Show your gratitude to clients, friends, family and peers by actively thanking them for being part of your journey. Make sure they know how much it means to you to have them on board. Clients provide your livelihood, those close to you cheer you on all the way and offer shoulder to cry on. Thank them, and thank them often.

List the people you want to thank

Habit tracker   •   •   •   •   •   •   •   •   •

Mood tracker   ☀   ☾   Sleep   ☀   :   ☾   :

Today, I am greatful for .....

Notes and reflections

Notes and reflections

Notes and reflections

about

Radim Malinic is a creative director, designer and bestselling author. He lives and works in south west London, where he runs his award-winning branding and creative studio Brand Nu.

Before finding his calling in the creative industry, Czech-born Malinic was an ice hockey player, a bassist in death metal bands, an indie DJ, a music journalist and a student of economics and business management. At the break of the new millennium, Malinic moved to the UK to explore its expansive music scene, only to find even a greater interest in art and graphic design. Since then his eclectic interests have seen him working with some of the biggest brands, companies and bands in the world. Clients include Harry Potter, London Film Museum, Decleor, Adidas, Dolby, WWF and USAID amongst many others.

Having been interested in mindfulness and meditation since his early teens, Malinic immersed himself fully in the practices following a series of burnouts he experienced during his ongoing career in the creative industry. All published titles by Malinic feature new ways to approach mindful creativity and business life.

For more information visit **brandnu.co.uk** or **radimmalinic.co.uk**

•

Adiba Osmani is the founder of Inhere, London's first dedicated drop-in meditation studio, which offers classes, talks and bespoke meditation pods. She teaches and speaks about meditation widely, and has been featured by The Times, The Guardian and the BBC for bringing meditation to schools, offices and audiences around the world.

Osmani studied philosophy at Oxford University before spending the following two decades working in branding and marketing for both large corporations and startups. She now runs Inhere with the intention to help people develop healthy relationships with their minds.

For more information, please visit **inherestudio.com**

available book series

by Radim Malinic

Book of Ideas - Vol.1
A journal of creative direction
and graphic design
ISBN 978-0-9935400-0-4
(OUT NOW)

Book of Ideas - Vol.2
A journal of creative direction
and graphic design
ISBN 978-0-9935400-1-1
(OUT NOW)

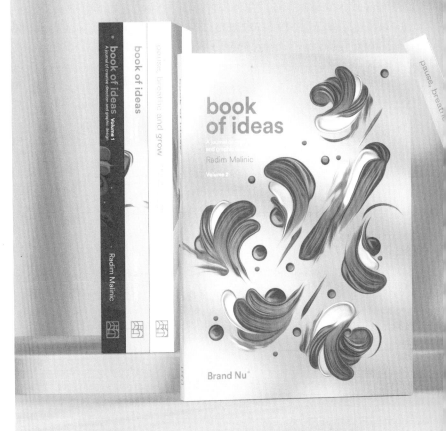

Book of Visual
Storytelling
for Brands
ISBN 978-0-9935400-4-2
(COMING SOON)

Book of Branding
a guide to creating brand identity
for startups and beyond
ISBN 978-0-9935400-3-5
(OUT NOW)

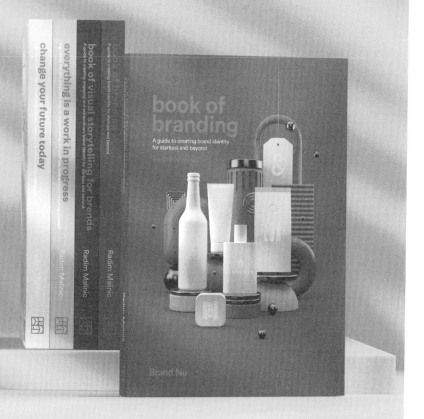

191

bonus content
and download

This book comes with bonus downloadable content, including:

- Guided audio meditations by Adiba Osmani
- A bonus Pause, Breathe and Grow PDF book
  of extra prompts
- Wallpaper images featured in the book for use
  across desktops or smartphones

To access these, visit **pausebreathegrow.com** and follow the instructions.

All content will be delivered to your inbox for you to enjoy.